GRI

Origins

Animals in Danger

Alison Hawes

Contents

Life on Earth	2
Finding new animals	4
How animals are lost	6
A–C	8
D–F	10
G–I	12
J–K	14
L–N	16
O–Q	18
R–S	20
T–U	22
X–W	24
Y–Z	26
Saving species	28
Quick quiz	30
Glossary	31
Index	32

Life on Earth

Our planet is bursting with life! Scientists think there are about 8.7 million different types of living things on Earth. Most of these are animals.

Lost and found

It's hard to know exactly how many types of animals there are on Earth because the number changes all the time. Thousands of amazing new animal **species** are found every year. Sadly, thousands more are lost when they become **extinct**.

Home Sweet Home

Keeping track

Keeping track of all those different animals is really tricky. To make it easier, scientists sort similar animals into groups. So far, about 1.8 million different kinds of animals have been named and sorted. Scientists think it could take 1000 years to find, sort and name the rest!

Animal groups

Animals can be classified into two main groups: vertebrates (animals with backbones) and invertebrates (animals without backbones). Within these groups, animals can be sorted into smaller groups, called classes.

Vertebrates

- **Mammals**

Find out about my funny sneezes on page 21.

- **Fish**

Find out what I am as flat as on page 16.

- **Amphibians**

Find out about my strange nose on page 18.

- **Reptiles**

Find out why I have disappeared on page 9.

- **Birds**

Find out why I couldn't fly on page 10.

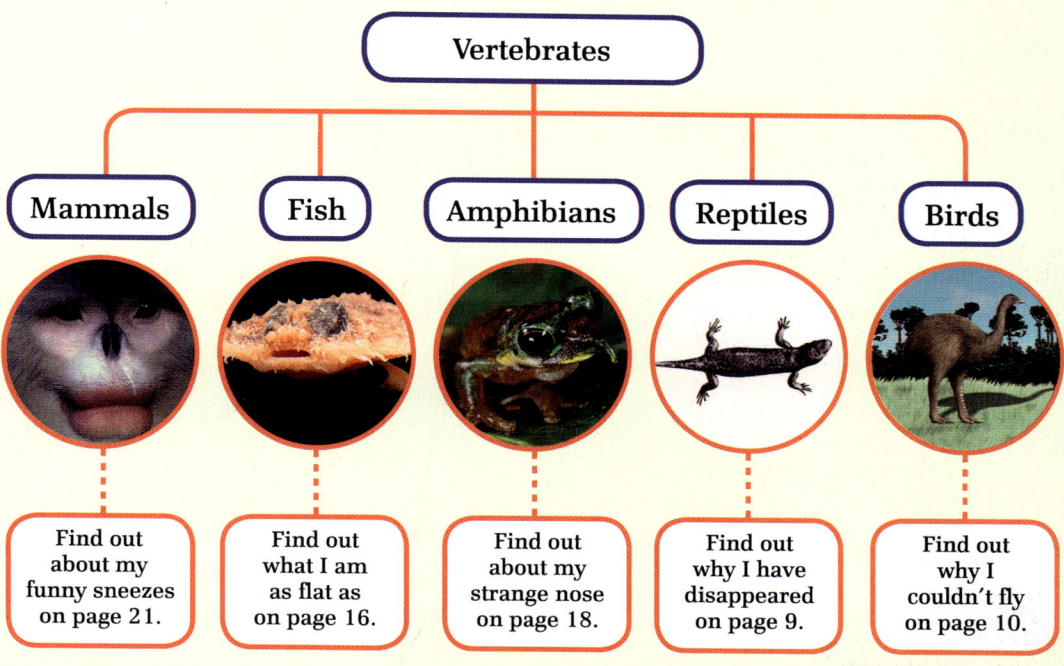

DID YOU KNOW?

97% of animal species are invertebrates!

Finding new animals

Around 15 000 new animal species are discovered and named each year. So where have they all been hiding?

New discoveries

Most new animal species are found in remote, hard-to-reach places on land and in the sea. Some are discovered accidentally by ordinary people, such as fishermen or hunters. Most are found by scientists on special expeditions to find new species.

Exploring the oceans

The sea covers most of the planet but it is so vast and deep that 90% of it has yet to be explored. Scientists can now go deeper into the ocean than ever before, with remotely operated vehicles, called **ROVs**.

The ROV can photograph and collect new animals for scientists to study.

DID YOU KNOW?

99% of the living space on Earth is underwater! That's why it is often called the blue planet.

Exploring the land

George McGavin is a **zoologist**. He goes on expeditions to find new animals in remote places. He especially loves finding new creepy-crawlies! He has had several insects named after him.

A shield bug from Borneo (in the photo above), a cockroach from South East Asia, a planthopper and an ant from Africa have all been named after George McGavin.

Exploring the past

It is not just new living animals that are found every year. Sometimes the fossils of unknown extinct animals are found, too.

VECTIDRACO DAISYMORRISAE

19th March 2013

Nine-year-old Daisy Morris heard today that an animal she discovered in 2009 is to be named in her honour. Daisy was just five when she found the fossil of this prehistoric flying reptile on a beach in the UK.

Vectidraco daisymorrisae

How animals are lost

Right now, more than 3000 species of animals are in danger of becoming extinct. We say these animals are endangered.

Animals in danger

Every year, people interested in helping endangered animals draw up an important list. They call it the Red List. It sorts animals and plants into seven groups, depending on how close to extinction they are.

The scimitar-horned oryx was reintroduced to Souss Massa National park in Morocco but it is extinct in the wild.

The Red List groups

1. Animals that are extinct
2. Animals that are extinct in the wild. Species in this group only exist in **captivity**.
3. 4. 5. Animals that are in danger of becoming extinct.
6. 7. Animals that are not in danger.

Watch out for humans!

There are various reasons why animals become endangered. For many species, the main reason is human activity.

Sometimes humans:

- destroy the places where animals live
- hunt animals, for instance for their fur, horns or meat
- pollute the air, land and water where animals live.

If nothing is done to help them, endangered animals can quickly become extinct.

Plastic bottles and other rubbish washed up on the coast of Palau Bunaken.

DID YOU KNOW?

Over 99% of all animal species that have ever lived on our planet are already extinct.

Read on to embark on a journey through an A–Z of weird and wonderful animals, lost and found, from all over the world.

African Coelacanth

(see-la-can-th)

This gigantic bony fish died out at the same time as the dinosaurs. Or so scientists thought, until one turned up in a fisherman's net in South Africa in 1938! The fish may have survived for so long partly because they are not very good to eat. Their oily skin and flesh taste foul!

Fast Facts

Group:	Vertebrates
Class:	Fish
Food:	Other fish
Habitat:	Deep underwater caves off South and east African coasts, and in the West Indian Ocean

Coelacanth can grow up to 2 metres long!

FOUND 3

Bearded Titi
(tee-tee)

Fast Facts
Group:	Vertebrates
Class:	Mammals
Food:	Fruit, leaves, seeds
Habitat:	Rainforest

In 2008, a group of scientists ventured deep into the Amazon rainforest. They had heard reports that a monkey with a bushy red beard had been spotted! Using **GPS technology**, they searched on foot and eventually found several groups of these strange-looking monkeys.

Baby bearded titi monkeys purr like cats!

FOUND 3

Cape Verde Giant Skink

Fast Facts
Group:	Vertebrates
Class:	Reptiles
Food:	Eggs, birds and plants
Habitat:	Trees on the Cape Verde islands

A living Cape Verde giant skink has not been seen for more than 70 years. This may be because humans hunted the skink for food and medicine, and destroyed its habitat.

Some believe that **droughts** also led to the giant skink becoming extinct.

LOST 1

DID YOU KNOW?

In 1833, one of the islands where the skink lived was used as a prison. Prisoners were left on the island, without any food. They ate every giant skink they could find!

Darth Vader jellyfish

Fast Facts
Group:	Invertebrates
Class:	Jellyfish
Food:	Fish
Habitat:	Arctic Ocean

These tiny jellyfish glow in the dark. They were found in 2005 by scientists looking for new animals in the Arctic Ocean. Using an ROV, scientists dived 1.6 km under the surface and photographed hundreds of these weird jellies for the first time.

These jellyfish really do look like the *Star Wars* film villain, Darth Vader.

FOUND 3

Elephant bird

Fast Facts
Group:	Vertebrates
Class:	Bird
Food:	Grass leaves and shoots
Habitat:	Forests by the sea in Madagascar

These enormous birds were hunted for their meat and eggs. Just one egg could feed a family for days. The birds were very easy to catch because they were too heavy to fly. They were eventually hunted to extinction.

Elephant birds laid eggs 100 times bigger than a hen's egg.

LOST 1

Falkland Islands wolf

Fast Facts
Group:	Vertebrates
Class:	Mammals
Food:	Birds and insects
Habitat:	Rocky grassland on the Falkland Islands

Falkland Islands wolves were so tame they would eat out of a person's hand! Sadly, this made them easy to hunt for their valuable fur.

The famous scientist Charles Darwin visited the Falkland Islands 180 years ago, when the wolves were still alive. This is what he wrote in his journal:

> They have been observed to enter a tent, and actually pull some meat from beneath the head of a sleeping seaman. The Gauchos also have frequently in the evening killed them, by holding out a piece of meat in one hand, and in the other a knife ready to stick them ... Their numbers have rapidly decreased ... Within a very few years after these islands shall have become regularly settled, in all probability this [wolf] will be classed with the dodo, as an animal which has perished from the face of the Earth.

The first recorded sighting of a Falkland Islands wolf was in 1690.

LOST 1

Giant stick insect

Fast Facts
Group:	Invertebrates
Class:	Insects
Food:	Leaves
Habitat:	Trees and bushes

There were once so many giant stick insects on Lord Howe Island, they were used as fishing bait. After rats escaped on to the island from a wrecked ship, the stick insects disappeared. They were thought to have become extinct. Amazingly, 80 years later, 24 were found alive.

Finding the stick insects wasn't easy. They live on the tallest, most isolated **sea-stack** in the world!

DID YOU KNOW?

Two scientists used climbing gear to reach the stick insects. They had to search in the dark when the insects were active.

The Lord Howe Island stick insect is one of the rarest insects in the world!

FOUND 3

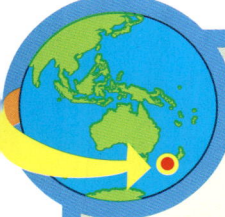

Haast's eagle

Fast Facts
Group:	Vertebrates
Class:	Birds
Food:	Birds and mammals
Habitat:	Dense forest on the south island of New Zealand

These huge eagles dive-bombed their **prey**, like hang-gliders with claws! Swooping down at 80 kph, they killed giant Moa birds with a powerful blow to the head or neck. When the Moas were hunted to extinction by humans, the eagles died out too.

Haast's eagles were the largest **raptors** that ever lived. Females were larger than males and were thought to weigh 10–15 kg!

LOST 1

Icefish

Fast Facts
Group:	Vertebrates
Class:	Fish
Food:	**Krill** and small fish
Habitat:	Cold seas

In 2009, scientists working in the Antarctic Sea found many bizarre-looking creatures. Among them was this strange, see-through fish. Icefish swim quite happily in the icy Antarctic waters because their blood contains a **chemical** that stops it freezing.

FOUND 7

Icefish have yellow blood.

13

Javan elephant
(jah-vun)

Fast Facts

Group:	Vertebrates
Class:	Mammals
Food:	Leaves, bark and root
Habitat:	Rainforest in Java and Borneo

For many years, scientists thought the **pygmy** Javan elephant was extinct. However, in 2008 they found some living in Borneo, an island 1300 km away from the elephants' home island of Java. How they had managed to get to Borneo is a mystery.

Javan elephants are called 'pygmy' elephants because they are smaller than African and Indian elephants.

DID YOU KNOW?

In the past, elephants were sent as presents from one Asian ruler to another. Scientists think the Javan elephant may have been saved from extinction when a herd was sent to the ruler of Borneo as a gift, hundreds of years ago.

FOUND 3

'Killer' kangaroos

Fast Facts

Group:	Vertebrates
Class:	Mammals
Food:	Meat
Habitat:	Rainforest in Australia

In 2006, Australian scientists discovered a new kind of kangaroo. They called it the 'killer' kangaroo. It had fangs and long arms, and ate meat rather than plants.

Don't panic! These kangaroos lived about 10 million years ago. Only their **fossilized** bones have been found.

The killer kangaroo didn't hop like the kangaroos of today. They galloped after their prey!

FOUND 1

Louisiana Pancake Batfish
(loo-eez-i-ana)

Fast Facts

Group:	Vertebrates
Class:	Fish
Food:	Small animals
Habitat:	Sea bed in the Gulf of Mexico

This weird fish crawls across the ocean floor on its fins. Louisiana Pancake Batfish were discovered in 2010. Shortly after, the sea where they live was polluted by a giant oil spill. Scientists are scared that the oil will harm the fish and even make it extinct – just after it's been found.

The Louisiana Pancake Batfish is well named. It's found in Louisiana, USA, and is as flat as a pancake!

FOUND 7

What's in a name?
The Louisiana Pancake Batfish was named after its habitat and the way it looks. How did some of the other animals in this book get their names?

Location	Sound	Person	Looks
Javan Elephant	Sneezing Monkey	Zuniceratops	Pinocchio Frog
Cape Verde Giant Skink	Quagga	Haast's Eagle	Darth Vader Jellyfish
Tasmanian Tiger			Yeti Crab
Giant Réunion Tortoise			Vampire Squid

Martinique giant rat
(mar-tin-eek)

Fast Facts	
Group:	Vertebrates
Class:	Mammals
Food:	Grasses, fruit and seeds
Habitat:	Forest and **plantations** in Martinique

The Martinique giant rat was once considered a tasty meal – after it had been boiled twice to get rid of its nasty smell! Some people think this giant rat was wiped out when a volcano erupted on Martinique in 1902. Others think that mongooses brought to the island hunted the rats to extinction.

This giant rat was the size of a cat!

LOST 1

Negros flying fox
(ne-ross)

Fast Facts	
Group:	Vertebrates
Class:	Mammals
Food:	Fruit
Habitat:	Small forest caves on Negros Island and Cebu Island

There used to be so many of these megabats on the island of Negros that the islanders used the bat poo as a **fertilizer**! However, the bats vanished when the rainforest they lived in was cut down. Then in 2003, scientists were amazed to find five still living on the island.

Their habitat is still under threat from **poaching** and forest destruction.

FOUND 3

17

Okapi
(oe-ka-pee)

An okapi's blue tongue is so long, it can lick its ears clean!

Okapi are so shy, they are rarely spotted in the wild. For 50 years, they were thought to be extinct in part of the Congo in West Africa. Then in 2008, scientists finally caught one on camera!

Fast Facts

Group:	Vertebrates
Class:	Mammals
Food:	Grass, leaves, fruit and **fungi**
Habitat:	Rainforest in the Democratic Republic of Congo

FOUND 6

Pinocchio frog
(pin-o-kee-oe)

Fast Facts

Group:	Vertebrates
Class:	Amphibians
Food:	Insects
Habitat:	Rainforest in the Foja mountains of Indonesia

In 2008, a group of scientists was looking for new kinds of animals in the Indonesian rainforest when this strange frog hopped into their camp and sat on a bag of rice. The scientists looked for more frogs like it. This was the only one they found.

The Pinocchio frog's nose inflates as it croaks!

FOUND 7

Quagga
(kwa-ga)

Fast Facts

Group:	Vertebrates
Class:	Mammals
Food:	Grass
Habitat:	Grasslands of South Africa

Quaggas looked like the front of a zebra stuck to the back of a horse! They had excellent hearing, which kept them safe from most **predators**. However, nothing could keep them safe from the humans who hunted them to extinction.

This is the world's only photograph of a live quagga. It was taken at London Zoo in 1870.

LOST 1

Back from the dead

Once an animal is extinct, it can't come back. Or can it? Scientists have been trying to bring back the quagga since 1987. They chose zebras with light stripes, like those the quagga had. Then they bred these animals until finally a foal was born that looked just like a quagga. Is it really a quagga or is it just a lookalike?

Henry was the first foal to be born in 2005.

19

Réunion giant tortoise
(ree-ue-nee-on)

Fast Facts	
Group:	Vertebrates
Class:	Reptiles
Food:	Leaves and fruit
Habitat:	Island of Réunion

Réunion giant tortoises could go for months without food and water. This might sound like a good way to survive but it was the reason the animals became extinct. Hundreds of years ago, sailors stopped at Réunion Island to load tortoises on to their ships. They knew the tortoises would stay alive on long journeys so the crew would have fresh meat to eat. Eventually, they ate them all and the tortoises became extinct.

These tortoises could grow to be 1.3 metres long!

LOST 1

There are vast numbers of tortoises here. Their flesh is very delicate and their fat better than butter.

Old documents can help scientists find out why animals became extinct. A traveller to Réunion Island wrote this in 1650.

These tortoises are found at the top of a mountain, which is covered in them. There were even more, but many have been destroyed. There is now a shortage.

Just 50 years later, another traveller wrote this.

Snub-nosed monkey

Fast Facts

Group:	Vertebrates
Class:	Mammals
Food:	Fruit and leaves
Habitat:	Forests in Myanmar

Scientists looking for new species in Myanmar were intrigued when local people told them about this monkey. They said it was easy to find: all the scientists had to do was wait until it rained. Then they would hear the monkeys sneezing!

Snub-nosed monkeys live in large groups of around 600 monkeys!

DID YOU KNOW?

Snub-nosed monkeys have upturned noses that quickly fill with rainwater, making them sneeze. Locals say the monkeys sometimes sit with their head between their knees, to keep out the rain!

FOUND 3

21

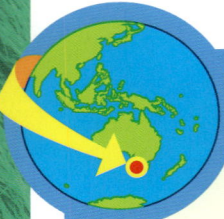

Tasmanian tiger

(taz-main-ee-un)

Fast Facts

Group:	Vertebrates
Class:	Mammals
Food:	Small animals and birds
Habitat:	Woodland in Tasmania

Tasmanian tigers were not really tigers. They were striped, dog-like **marsupials** that hunted at night. Like kangaroos, they had a pouch and could stand on their back legs. But like tigers, they were predators with no enemies except humans.

The Tasmanian tiger is extinct but some people say they are still alive and that they have seen them!

> We were driving along when we saw this animal crossing the road. It was about the size of a dog and we could see stripes on its rump.
>
> Andrew, 20th March 2009

> I could see this dog-like animal walking along the road. It then stood up like a kangaroo on its hind legs and then it got back down and started walking like a dog again.
>
> Diana, 30th January 2010

A Tasmanian tiger could open its mouth unusually wide.

LOST 1

Underwater harp

Fast Facts

Group:	Invertebrates
Class:	Sponges
Food:	Bacteria and floating organisms
Habitat:	Pacific Ocean

It's hard to believe that this strangely shaped animal is actually a meat-eating sponge! The harp sponge is shaped like a musical instrument called a harp. It was discovered off the coast of California, USA, in 2012.

Harp sponges as long as 60 cm have been found.

DID YOU KNOW?

Deadly Velcro
Harp sponges feed on bacteria and larger prey floating in the ocean. Their 'branches' are covered in tiny hooks, that stick to their prey like Velcro!

FOUND 7

23

Vampire Squid

Fast Facts

Group:	Invertebrates
Class:	Chephalopods
Food:	Debris on ocean floor
Habitat:	Deep seas

The vampire squid has probably been around for 165 million years. But this tiny red squid was only found about 100 years ago! It lives deep in the ocean where there is no natural light. Scientists have recently used ROVs to film it, hundreds of metres under the surface of the sea.

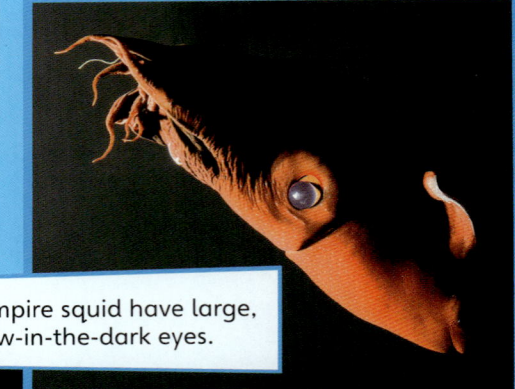

Vampire squid have large, glow-in-the-dark eyes.

arms

DID YOU KNOW?

When the squid escapes from predators, it pulls its arms back over itself. This makes it look like a vampire in a black cloak! It also makes the squid almost invisible in the dark water.

FOUND 7

24

Wasps

Fast Facts
- **Group:** Invertebrates
- **Class:** Insects
- **Food:** Nectar (as adults)
- **Habitat:** Grassland

These tiny wasps are barely 2mm long. However, they are not afraid of ants ten times their size. In fact, they go looking for them. When the wasp finds one, it dive-bombs the ant and injects an egg into its body. The ant then meets a gruesome end ...

1. The tiny wasp attacks the much bigger ant.
2. The wasp injects an egg into the ant's body.
3. The wasp's egg hatches inside the ant's body. The wasp's **larva** feeds on the ant from the inside out.

This dive-bombing wasp was discovered in Spain.

FOUND 7

Xenorhinotherium
(zen-oe-rhine-oe-theer-ium)

Fast Facts
Group:	Vertebrates
Class:	Mammals
Food:	Grass and leaves
Habitat:	Grassland in Brazil

Not only did this animal have a tiny trunk for a nose, its nostrils were on top of its head! Some scientists think it may have used its nose like a snorkel. We will never know for sure. Xenorhinotherium became extinct during the last ice age when the first humans appeared.

This animal's name means 'beast with a strange nose'.

LOST 1

Yeti crab
(yet-ee)

Fast Facts
Group:	Invertebrates
Class:	Crabs and relatives
Food:	Algae and small animals
Habitat:	Ocean floor around Easter Island

With its big hairy arms, this blind crab looks like it is trying to keep warm! The scientists who discovered it in 2005 say it lives next to jets of hot water that bubble up from the ocean floor.

This yeti crab is 15 cm long.

FOUND 7

Zuniceratops christopheri

(zoo-nee-sera-tops)

Fast Facts

Group:	Vertebrates
Class:	Reptiles
Food:	Plants
Habitat:	Hills and grassland in New Mexico, USA

In 1996, three brilliant things happened to eight-year-old Christopher Wolfe:

1. His dad took him fossil hunting.
2. Christopher found the bones of a dinosaur no one had seen before.
3. Scientists named the new dinosaur, after him.

Christopher's dinosaur was a cow-sized reptile. It lived in North America about 90 million years ago. It had two eyebrow horns, a frill behind its head and a beak for a mouth!

Christopher discovered the dinosaur in New Mexico.

Zuniceratops was approximately 3 metres tall.

FOUND 1

Saving species

Could you discover an animal that has never been found before? Or help to protect a species from becoming extinct?

Why do we need so many different types of animals?

Animals and plants are very important for the health of our planet. Without them, it would be impossible for us to survive! Humans depend on a wide variety of animals and plants. We need them for things such as food, clothing, clean water and medicine. This is one reason scientists are keen to discover new species – they could bring benefits we don't even know about.

What can be done to protect species?

Scientists fear that too many animals and plants are becoming extinct. Many zoos, wildlife groups and governments are trying to help endangered animals to survive. Banning hunting, protecting habitats and breeding animals in captivity are different ways people are trying to help animals survive.

Bao Bao was born at a zoo in America in August 2013.

How can zoos help animals?

Many animals, such as the Negros flying fox (page 17), could be saved by protecting their habitats. The rainforest where these bats once lived was cut down but now it is being replanted in some places.

Exploring the past

Other animals, such as the Lord Howe Island stick insect (page 12), are being saved from extinction by zoos. From just one pair of stick insects, an Australian zoo has bred hundreds more. Some of them have already been returned to live on Lord Howe Island.

Conservation work is good news for animals, good news for humans and good news for the planet.

A walking stick insect hatching from an egg.

Quick quiz

So how much have you learned? Do you know your African Coelacanth from your Zuniceratops christopheri? Try our short quiz to find out.

If you need help with any answers, turn to the page given for each question.

1. Why does the number of animals on Earth keep changing? (Page 2)
2. What are the two main groups animals can be sorted into? (Page 3)
3. What does the Red List tell us? (Page 6)
4. Which animal looks like a *Star Wars* villain? (Page 10)
5. Why did the Haast's eagle become extinct? (Page 13)
6. How do 'killer' kangaroos differ from today's kangaroos? (Page 15)
7. What did the Negros islanders use bat poo for? (Page 17)
8. Why do sneezing monkeys try to avoid the rain? (Page 21)
9. What do harp sponges feed on? (Page 23)
10. How are Lord Howe stick insects being helped to survive? (Page 29)

Glossary

captivity — kept locked up, unable to leave

chemical — a compound or substance, e.g. starch

drought — low rainfall which means there is not enough water

endangered — at risk of extinction

extinct — no members of the species alive

fertilizer — something added to soil to help crops grow

fossilized — changed into a fossil

fungi — (plural of fungus) a group of plants including mushrooms and toadstools

GPS technology — (Global Positioning System) a way of navigating using satellites

krill — a small plankton found in the sea

larva — the young form of an insect which often doesn't look like the adult form, e.g. a caterpillar

marsupial — a mammal that carries its young in a pouch, e.g. a kangaroo

nectar — a sugary liquid found in flowers

plantation — a type of farm where crops like coffee and sugar are grown

poaching — hunting animals illegally

predator — an animal that lives by killing and eating other animals

prey — an animal that is hunted

pygmy — a word to discribe something small

raptor — a bird of prey, e.g. an eagle

ROV — a remotely operated vehicle

sea-stack — a column of rock standing in the sea

species — a group of creatures that are the same, e.g. lion

zoologist — someone who studies animals

Index

amphibians 3, 18

birds 3, 9, 10-11, 13, 22

endangered 6-7, 28

extinct/extinction 2, 5, 6-7, 10, 12-13, 14, 16-20, 22, 26, 28-29

fish 3, 8, 10, 13,

found 2, 4-5, 7, 8-10, 12–18, 20-21, 23, 24-28

insects 5, 11, 12, 25, 29

invertebrates 3, 10, 12, 23, 24-25, 26

lost 2, 6, 7, 9, 10-11, 13, 17, 19, 20, 22, 26,

mammals 3, 9, 11, 13, 14-15, 17, 18-19, 21, 22, 26

reptiles 3, 9, 20

ROV 4, 10, 24

scientists 2-4, 8-10, 13, 14-21, 24, 26-28

vertebrates 3, 8, 9-11, 13-21, 22, 24, 26-27

Quick quiz answers:

1. New ones are discovered whilst others become extinct.; 2. Vertebrates and invertebrates.; 3. How close animals and plants are to extinction.; 4. Darth Vader Jellyfish.; 5. Its prey became extinct.; 6. They had fangs and long arms, and ate meat rather than plants.; 7. Fertilizer.; 8. Rain water gets in their noses and makes them sneeze.; 9. Bacteria and larger prey floating in the ocean.; 10. Australian zoos are breeding them.